My Party
Art Class

Nellie Shepherd

A Dorling Kindersley Book

LONDON, NEW YORK, MUNICH, MELBOURNE, AND DELHI

Editor Penny Smith
Senior Designer Wendy Bartlet
Designer Victoria Long
Additional Design Melanie Leighton
Production Shivani Pandey
Photography Stephen Hepworth

For David Hansel (A Wonderful Party Animal!)

ACKNOWLEDGMENTS
With thanks to: Jean Gollner, Anne Lumb, David Hansel (Memery Crystal), James Merifield,
Joseph Whitworth Centre, and all the children who took part in the photography.
Special thanks to the artists: Kathleen Bailey, Victoria Long, Jane McDonald,
Katie Noorlander, James Pendrich, and Amy McSimpson.

First published in Great Britain in 2004
by Dorling Kindersley Limited
80 Strand, London WC2R ORL
A Penguin Company
2 4 6 8 10 9 7 5 3 1

A CIP catalogue record for this book
is available from the British Library

ISBN: 1-4053-0417-0

Colour reproduction by GRB Editrice, Italy
Printed and bound in China by Toppan

See
Dorling Kindersley's
complete catalogue at
www.dk.com

It's party time!

Introduction and Party Planner

pages 4 – 7

Underwater Party
Pages 8 – 23

Garden Party
Pages 24 – 35

Magic Party
Pages 36 – 47

My Party Art Class

This book is filled with ideas for art parties, where children make fantastic creations!

I love arty parties – I must do, I've organized over 800 and still counting! Themed parties work best, so in this book I've put together ideas for three themed arty parties. Children make at least two projects, then take their wonderful art home. They feel they've achieved something – and had a brilliant time too! And to cut down on mess, all the projects in this book are paint-free. Go on – go for it!

Love
Nellie x

Find out about planning a party on page 6.

4

Basic kit

Here's a useful art kit. Add other things to it as you try each project, and remember – if you don't have something, just improvise!

scissors
felt-tip pens
PVA glue
stapler
cellophane
card
pipe cleaners
sticky-back
  paper
tissue paper
shiny paper
stickers

masking tape
double-sided
  tape
net fabric
felt
glitter
paintbrushes

Keep your art kit in a box so you can find it easily!

Helping hand

All the projects in this book are designed for young children to make, but they should only be attempted under adult supervision. Extra care should be taken when using sharp equipment, such as scissors, staplers, and pipe cleaners, and with small objects that may cause choking. Only use PVA or other non-toxic, water-soluble glue.

Party Planner

For a great arty party, it's a must to be organized! Send out invitations three weeks before the party, and make sure you have everything you need well in advance. Then create and have fun!

Guest numbers
depend on how much room you have. For a home party, where space is limited, anything from 6 to 12 children works well. In a hired venue you can invite the whole class.

A timetable
is essential! In my experience the perfect party lasts 2 hours – 10 minutes to settle in, 1 hour to make things, 20 minutes for tea, then 30 minutes of party games.

Little ones
need lots of help! Prepare the basic craft projects before the party, so all children have to do is decorate them. And prepare a few extra for surprise guests!

Protect the floor

with cheap wallpaper lining paper, taped in place with masking tape.

Play music,

the more funky and upbeat the better! It makes a huge difference to the atmosphere. Children lose themselves in the art, while bopping to the music.

Lay out

the craft materials for each child on the covered floor. Show everyone what they are going to make and how to make it, then let them get stuck in!

Games

work best when they're non-competitive. Musical statues is great to play – no one needs to be out, and it's so funny when you pretend you can't see children moving!

To end a party,

I burst balloons which I've filled with tissue confetti. The confetti falls like snow. It's magical and dramatic!

Underwater Party

Why not have a wonderful underwater party? Here children can dress up as mermaids or octopuses and make their very own jellyfish friends! They can play the great game of pass the puffer fish, and have a hilarious time doing the hokey cokey – their octopus legs fly everywhere!

You can make...

- Fishy Invitations

- Pass the Puffer Fish

- Shell Party Bags

- Adelaide the Mermaid

- Octopus Mo

- Jellyfish Friends

Get Started!

Fishy Invitations

Make a splash with these fishy invites! To make them, cut fish shapes from card, then glue on felt faces, scales, and fins. Write the time and place of your party on the back of each invitation.

Come to my party on... at...

Pass the Puffer Fish

In this fantastic version of pass the parcel, everyone wins! Inside a giant puffer fish are lots of little fish with presents inside them. Each time the music stops, a child wins a little fish.

I'm a little fish!

Make your little fish (look top right to see how). Wrap one little fish in a layer of paper. Add another little fish and another layer of paper and so on, until you have one big parcel full of little fish. Decorate your final layer to look like a big puffer fish with craft-ball eyes, card eyelashes, and sticky-back paper lips.

Little Fish

To make a little fish, put a gift in a small cardboard tube. Wrap the tube in paper, then tuck one end of the paper into the tube. Tie the other end with ribbon for the fish's tail. Decorate with shiny paper fins and wiggly eyes.

Shell Party Bags

Wow your guests with pretty party bags! For each one, cut a paper plate into a shell shape. Glue on strips of cellophane, tissue paper, and beads. Then stick your shell onto a paper party bag. Sea-themed party gifts can include sunglasses, pots of bubbles, and even rubber ducks!

Adelaide the Mermaid

tissue paper

glitter

Adelaide
Is a mermaid,
Who lives
In the sea so blue.
When you make
Her fish's tail
You'll be
A mermaid, too!

You can use...

paper bowl

bubble wrap

pom-poms

glitter

ribbon

tissue paper

coloured sand

Tot Tip! For great party hats, make a starfish headband from a paper bowl and card, or a card crown. Decorate them with shiny paper, glitter, or pom-poms.

13

How to make it!

draw

Start by drawing two fish-tail shapes on bubble wrap and cutting them out.

tape

Cut out a rectangle of bubble wrap that's big enough to fit around your body like a skirt. Tape your fish tails to it.

stick

Paint glue over your fish-tail skirt and stick on lots of fish scales or other shapes cut from tissue paper. Sprinkle on coloured sand, or my favourite – glitter!

Hello!

staple

Finish your fish-tail skirt by stapling a length of ribbon to each top corner. Then tie it around your tummy.

Party tip
It's fun when
everyone
blows bubbles.
See if you can
catch one.

Octopus Mo

Pretend you are Mo,
The Octopus.
You really do look great.
Instead of having two legs,
Suddenly you have eight!

I'm all legs!

cake case

tights

You can use...

four pairs
of tights

cake cases

bubble wrap
or newspaper

Tot Tip! There's no need to spend a fortune on tights to make Octopus Mo. Outgrown or holey ones are perfect.

You can do it!

roll

Cut six bubble-wrap rectangles as long as the legs of your tights and roll them up. Or you can scrunch up newspaper to stuff your tights.

stuff

Now stuff the bubble wrap or newspaper as far into your tights as you can manage.

tie

Tie up the top of each pair of stuffed tights. Then make a skirt of legs by tying all the stuffed tights together.

Nice legs!

tape

Tape on little cake cases to look like octopus suckers. Put on the fourth pair of tights and wear the leggy skirt around your waist.

Party tip
This is the best outfit in the world to wear for the hokey cokey!

19

Jellyfish Friends

Here are two jolly jellyfish,
Each made from a balloon.
They're wibbly and wobbly
Like jelly on a spoon!

crepe paper

You can use...

crepe paper
or cellophane

balloon

sticky-back paper
or stickers

Tot Tip!

Balloons filled with helium make perfect floating jellyfish.
But you can also use ordinary air-filled balloons –
simply hang them from string and decorate them.

Here we go!

stick

Start making your jellyfish by sticking double-sided tape around a balloon. Once it's stuck, leave it there or your balloon will burst!

stick again

Stick long strips of crepe paper or cellophane onto the double-sided tape so the strips hang down like jellyfish tentacles.

draw

Draw shapes on sticky-back paper and cut them out (or you can use stickers). Stick the shapes all over your jellyfish to make it really beautiful.

I'm a great playmate!

finish

To finish, give your jellyfish a friendly face with lovely lips, eyes, and eyelashes.

Party tip
Make a few jellyfish before your party – you can give them to children who accidentally burst their balloons.

23

24

Garden Party

It's time for a tea party with a difference, so send out invitations to this wonderful arty garden party. You don't even need a garden! You can transform your home into a pretend garden, or have a party in the park. Children love making giant funky flowers and bright bumblebee hats – and a treasure hunt is a must!

You can make...

 Flower Invitations

 Ladybird Invitations

 Party Bunting

 Teapot Picnic Boxes

 Funky Flowers

 Boris the Bee

Flower Invitations

To make these gorgeous invitations, cut flower shapes from card. Decorate them with balls of scrunched-up tissue paper. For extra fun, stick a photocopied picture of yourself in the middle! Don't forget to write on party details.

Come to my party!

Party invite!

Ladybird Invitations

You need two paper plates to make a ladybird invitation. Cut one plate in half for the wings. Then decorate the plates with felt or paper and give your ladybird a felt face. Attach the ladybird's wings to its body using paper fasteners.

Party Bunting

For party bunting, fold paper napkins over a piece of ribbon. Use tape to hold each napkin together. It's as easy at that!

Teapot Picnic Boxes

To make each sparkly teapot picnic box, cut out a teapot shape from card. Cover it with lots of glitter, then stick it on a party picnic box. Fill each box with party food.

Funky Flowers

tissue paper

paper plate

crepe paper

These garden party flowers
Can be lots of different colours.
First you make your favourite one
And then make lots of others.

28

You can use...

paper plates

cellophane

cardboard tube or garden cane

tissue paper

crepe paper

glitter

Tot Tip!

If you use garden-cane flower stalks, you can push them into soil and the flowers stand up by themselves.

How to make it!

arrange

Make a simple flower shape by arranging paper plates around one in the middle. Stick plenty of tape to the plates to hold your flower together.

glue

Your paper-plate flower will look really beautiful when you glue on cellophane, scrunched-up tissue paper, and glitter.

tape

To make a flower stalk, tape a garden cane or cardboard tube to your flower. You can decorate the stalk with shiny paper.

cut

Cut streamers of crepe paper, tape them to the top of the stalk, and let them hang free.

31

Boris the Bee

pipe cleaner

tissue paper

This bee
Is called Boris.
He's really
Quite funny.
He flies through
The flowers,
Then goes home
To make honey.

32

You can use...

tissue paper

fluffy balls

felt

net fabric

pipe cleaners

card

Tot Tip! Boris's lovely bulgy eyes are easy to make using fluffy pom-poms or cotton-wool balls. Simply glue a circle of black felt in the middle of each one.

You can do it!

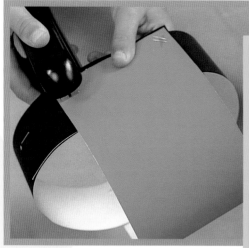

staple
To make Boris's body, staple a wide piece of card to a card headband.

stick
Stick a few strips of double-sided tape across Boris's body.

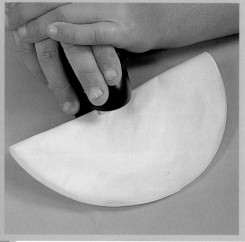

pile up
Now, pile up five tissue-paper circles. Staple them together in the middle.

scrunch
Scrunch each tissue-paper circle to make a flower.

attach
You'll need to make several flowers, then attach them to the double-sided tape across Boris's body. Add glitter, if you like.

cut

Cut wings from net fabric.
Gather up the net and tie
it with pipe cleaners.

staple again

Staple Boris's wings to his body.
Then staple on his pipe-cleaner
antennae, and glue on his eyes.

Magic Party

With this theme your party will fly by, especially with the help of a few helium balloons! Children can turn themselves into witches or wizards by making magical hats and cloaks. And they can even create their very own broomsticks to ride home on!

You can make...

★ Party Mural

★ Magical Cloak

★ Floating Balloons

★ Cauldron Party Bags

★ Flying Broomstick

★ Magic Mischief Hat

Party Mural

Tape together strips of wallpaper lining paper to make one large sheet. Then let everyone make a magical mural with glue, shiny stars, chalk, and lots of glitter!

Magical Cloak

This cloak is so easy to make, it's just like magic! Cut open a black bin liner, then cut it into the shape shown above to make a cloak with straps that tie round your neck. Glue paper stars and glitter to your cloak, then it's ready to wear!

Floating Balloons

It's worth buying a few helium-filled balloons to make these floating creations. Decorate them with sticky-back paper stars. Then tie ribbons to the balloons and staple paper stars and moons to the ribbons.

Cauldron Party Bags

For each party bag, cut out a card cauldron and decorate it with stars. Tape card stars to pipe cleaners and push them through your cauldron. Stick the cauldron to a paper bag. Great magic gifts include plastic wands, sticker stars, and chocolate frogs!

Flying Broomstick

Here's a magic broomstick.
It would really like to fly.
Fasten it to balloons,
Then point it to the sky.

I'm only here for the ride!

lagging pipe

pipe cleaner

card star

40

You can use...

cellophane

lagging pipe

pipe cleaners

card stars

shiny paper

crepe paper

Tot Tip! You can buy a lagging pipe from a hardware store. It doesn't cost much, and it is so light that a few helium balloons can hold it up in the air.

How to make it!

cover

Begin turning your lagging pipe into a broomstick by covering it with lots of lovely sticky glue.

wrap

Wrap strips of crepe paper or shiny paper around your broomstick. Keep your decoration as lightweight as you can.

sprinkle

For extra sparkle, sprinkle your broomstick with some gorgeous glitter.

stuff

Now stuff the end of your broomstick with lots of tissue paper, cellophane or net fabric, and pipe cleaners with card stars stapled to them.

Party tip
For a magical surprise, slip sweets into the end of each broomstick.

43

Magic Mischief Hat

A mischief hat
Is made from card
And shiny paper, too.
A wizard always wears one
When he plays
A trick on you!

pipe cleaners

shiny paper

card

44

You can use...

pipe cleaners

kitchen foil

ribbon

glitter

card

tissue paper

shiny paper

Tot Tip! If you want to make an incredibly neat pointed hat, cut out a card shape like the one shown here.

Here we go!

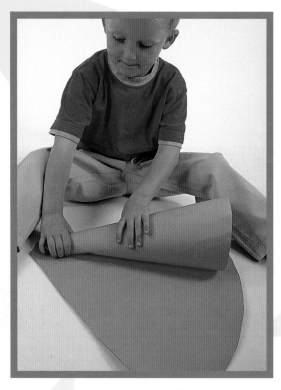

roll

This is an easy peasy project and it works brilliantly! Just roll up your card to make a cone-shaped hat.

stick

Check your hat fits, then stick on a few strips of tape to hold it together.

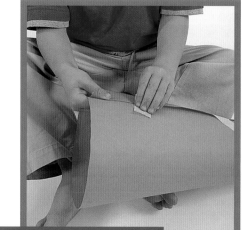

decorate

Decorate with shiny paper stars, kitchen foil or other shiny paper, tissue paper, or anything you like.

staple

Staple card stars to curled pipe cleaners. Staple the pipe cleaners to your hat.

attach

Attach two lengths of ribbon to your hat. Tie them under your chin and make mischief!

More Arty Parties

There are so many arty party themes that work brilliantly. Here are some to try using craft projects from my other books. Have fun!

My Art Class

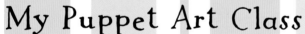

Sweetie Party

My Animal Art Class

Super Safari Party

My Puppet Art Class

A Puppet Party!

Yesssss!

My Picture Art Class

Flower Power Party